Instant Pot Cookbook

The Best Instant Pot Recipes for Your Whole Family

CHARLIE MASON

Charlie Mason

Copyright © 2017 Charlie Mason

The follow Book is reproduced below with the goal of providing information that is as accurate and reliable as possible. Regardless, purchasing this Book can be seen as consent to the fact that both the publisher and the author of this book are in no way experts on the topics discussed within and that any recommendations or suggestions that are made herein are for entertainment purposes only. Professionals should be consulted as needed prior to undertaking any of the action endorsed herein.

This declaration is deemed fair and valid by both the American Bar Association and the Committee of Publishers Association and is legally binding throughout the United States.

Furthermore, the transmission, duplication or reproduction of any of the following work including specific information will be considered an illegal act irrespective of if it is done electronically or in print. This extends to creating a secondary or tertiary copy of the work or a recorded copy and is only allowed with express written consent from the Publisher. All additional rights reserved.

The information in the following pages is broadly considered to be a truthful and accurate account of facts and as such any inattention, use or misuse of the information in question by the reader will render any resulting actions solely under their purview. There are no scenarios in which the publisher or the original author of this work can be in any fashion deemed liable for any hardship or damages that may befall them after undertaking information described herein.

Additionally, the information in the following pages is intended only for informational purposes and should thus be thought of as universal. As befitting its nature, it is presented without assurance regarding its prolonged validity or interim quality. Trademarks that are mentioned are done without written consent and can in no way be considered an endorsement from the trademark holder.

CONTENTS

1 Wholesome Breakfast Recipes to Get the Day Started   4

2 Lunch Recipes to Help Keep You Full   9

3 Snacks for the Middle of the Day   18

4 Delicious Desserts You are Going to Love   23

5 Conclusion   28

1 WHOLESOME BREAKFAST RECIPES TO GET THE DAY STARTED

Banana French Toast

What's in it

White sugar (1 Tbsp.)
Chopped pecans (4 Tbsp.)
Sliced butter (half a stick)
Cinnamon (.5 tsp.)
Vanilla (1 tsp.)
Milk (.5 c.)
Eggs (3)
Cream cheese (4 Tbsp.)
Brown sugar (2 Tbsp.)
Sliced bananas (4)
Cubed French bread (6 slices)

How's it done

1: Grease a baking dish or use a cake pan. Use a layer of the bread to the bottom and then layer half of the bananas on top.

2: Sprinkle a bit of brown sugar on top and then cover with the cream cheese before topping with the rest of the bread.

3: Add on the other half of the banana slices and sprinkle with some more brown sugar and the pecans. Place the slice dup butter on top.

4: In another bowl, beat the three eggs together before mixing the cinnamon, vanilla, white sugar, and milk inside as well. Pour this on top of the bread to coat.

5: Add some water to your instant pot and situation the steamer basket inside with the dish on top. Secure the lead and seal the pot up.

6: Select Manual and let the timer go for 5 minutes on a high pressure.

7: When this is done, use the quick pressure to release the lid and take it off the pot. Allow the bread to sit for a few minutes before serving.

Apple Oatmeal

What's in it

Chopped walnuts (2 Tbsp.)
Salt (.25 tsp.)
Brown sugar (1 Tbsp.)
Apple cider vinegar (1 tsp.)
Water (2 c.)
Cinnamon (1 tsp.)
Sliced apple (1)
Oats (1 c.)
Butter (2 Tbsp.)

How's it done

1: Select the Saute function on your instant pot and add in a bit of butter to the bottom. Let this melt before adding in the oats and cook for a few minutes.

2: After this time, add in the water, the brown sugar, apple cider vinegar, cinnamon, and apple.

3: Put the lid on securely and seal it all up. Click on manual and let this cook at a higher pressure for about 6 minutes.

4: When the time is up, allow for a natural release of the pressure and then open up the lid.

5: Move all the contents over to the bowl you want to serve in and then top with some walnuts before enjoying.

Breakfast Cobbler

What's in it

Sunflower seeds (2 Tbsp.)
Pecan pieces (.5 c.)
Shredded coconut (.5 c.)
Cinnamon (1 tsp.)
Coconut oil (4 Tbsp.)
Honey (4 Tbsp.)
Diced plums (2)
Diced apples (2)
Diced pears (2)

How's it done

1: Add the cinnamon, coconut oil, honey, diced plums, apples, and pears into the instant pot. Seal up the lid nice and tight.

2: Set this to a high pressure and let the ingredients cook together. After ten minutes, turn off the Instant pot and then use quick pressure release.

3: Open up the lid and then move the fruit over to a bowl, but do not get rid of the liquid.

4: Add in the sunflower seeds, pecans, and coconut to your pot and cook for another five minutes, making sure to stir this around often.

5: When this is done, turn the Instant Pot off and add the seeds over to the prepared fruits before serving.

Egg Bake

What's in it

Chopped green onions
Pepper (.5 tsp.)
Salt (1 tsp.)
Shredded cheddar cheese (.5 c.)
Milk (.25 c.)
Eggs (6)
Hash browns (2 c.)
Sliced mushrooms (1 c.)
Chopped onion (1)
Chopped bacon (6 slices)

How's it done

1: Take out a bowl that is heatproof and will fit into the Instant Pot.

2: Add in the bacon to the Instant Pot and cook to make crispy. Add in the mushrooms and onion and cook a bit before adding in the hash browns to thaw. Turn the Instant pot off.

3: In a bowl, mix the pepper, salt, cheddar cheese, milk, and eggs together. Add in the veggie mixture and the bacon mixture as well.

4: When these are combined, move it all to the bowl you picked out before.

5: Add some water to the Instant Pot before placing the trivet inside and the bowl on top. Secure the lid of the Instant Pot properly.

6: Cook this on a high pressure. After ten minutes are up, turn your Instant Pot off and then release the pressure.

7: Transfer the ingredients inside onto a plate and garnish with the green onions before serving.

Egg Muffins

What's in it

Chopped green onion (1)
Crumbled bacon (4 slices)
Shredded cheddar (4 Tbsp.)
Lemon pepper seasoning (.25 tsp.)
Eggs (4)

How's it done

1: Add a bit of water to your Instant Pot along with a steamer basket.

2: Take out a bowl and beat the eggs with the lemon pepper seasoning. Divide the green onion, bacon, and cheese between four muffin cups.

3: Add the eggs on top of the cups and then stir around a bit before adding into the Instant Pot.

4: Secure the lid well and then let this cook on a high pressure. After eight minutes are up, turn the pressure cooker off and give it some time for the pressure to release.

5: Take the lid off the Instant Pot and then take the muffin cups out to serve.

Sausage Frittata

What's in it

Pepper
Salt
Cooked sausage (.5 c.)
Cheddar cheese (4 Tbsp.)
Sour cream (2 Tbsp.)
Beaten eggs (4)
Water (2 c.)
Coconut oil (1 Tbsp.)

How's it done

1: Use a bit of coconut oil to grease up a baking dish. Add the water to the Instant Pot and then add in a steam basket as well.

2: Whisk together the sour cream and the eggs until well combined. Then stir in the pepper, salt, sausage, and cheese. Stir before pouring into the baking dish.

3: Use some foil to cover up the dish and then place inside of the Instant Pot. Close the lid and let this cook on a low pressure.

4: After 20 minutes, use a quick release pressure before opening up the Instant Pot. Top this dish with some more cheese before serving.

Tomato and Spinach Quiche

What's in it

Parmesan cheese (4 Tbsp.)
Tomato slices (4)
Chopped green onions (2)
Diced tomatoes (.5 c.)
Spinach (1.5 c.)
Pepper
Salt
Milk (.25 c.)
Eggs (6)

How's it done

1: Add a trivet to the bottom of your Instant Pot along with some water.

2: In a bowl, whisk together the pepper, salt, milk, and eggs until well combined.

3: Take out a baking dish and add in the green onions, tomatoes, and spinach to mix well. Top with your egg mixture and then place the sliced tomatoes on top with some Parmesan cheese.

4: Place the prepared baking dish on the trivet in the Instant Pot. Turn this on a high pressure.

5: After twenty minutes, turn the Instant Pot off and let the pressure release a bit. Open the lid and take the baking dish out before serving.

2 LUNCH RECIPES TO HELP KEEP YOU FULL

Vegetable and Beef Soup

What's in it

Oregano (.5 tsp.)
Parsley (2 tsp.)
Pepper
Salt
Tomato paste (3 Tbsp.)
Cubed potatoes (2)
Sliced celery (3)
Sliced carrots (4)
Stewed tomatoes (1 can)
Minced garlic cloves (4)
Diced onion (1)
Beef (2 lbs.)

How's it done

1: Turn on the Instant Pot to Saute. Add in the garlic, onion, and ground beef and keep cooking until the beef is browned. When it is done, drain off the grease.

2: Add in the stewed tomatoes and cook a bit longer.

3: After a few minutes add in the rest of the ingredients and then place the lid on top. Cook at a high pressure.

4: After four minutes are up, use the quick release method to get rid of the pressure. Move the soup over to some serving bowls before enjoying.

Chicken Noodle

What's in it

Parsley (4 Tbsp.)
Egg noodles (4 oz.)
Pepper (.5 tsp.)
Water (8 c.)
Soy sauce (2 Tbsp.)
Whole chicken (1)
Sliced celery (2)
Carrots (4)
Minced garlic cloves (4)

Diced onion (1)
Olive oil (1 Tbsp.)

How's it done

1: To preheat the Instant Pot, turn it on to Saute and then add in the olive oil. When this is hot, cook the onion for a bit and add in the celery, carrots, and garlic.

2: Add the chicken into the Instant Pot as well as the pepper, salt, soy sauce, water. Place the lid on top and seal the lid.

3: Cook this on a high pressure. After twenty minutes, quickly release the pressure and open the lid. Take the chicken out and shred it up.

4: Turn the heat back on with the Instant Pot and let this broth come to a boil. Add in the egg noodles and let them cook until soft.

5: Shred up the chicken into smaller pieces, getting rid of the skin and bone. Stir it back into the broth.

6: Adjust the seasonings how you would like and enjoy.

Cheesy Potato Soup

What's in it

Corn (1 c.)
Half and half (2 c.)
Shredded cheese (1 c.)
Cubed cream cheese (3 oz.)
Cornstarch mixed with water (2 Tbsp. each)
Parsley (2 Tbsp.)
Pepper
Salt
Chicken broth (2 c.)
Cubed potatoes (4)
Chopped onion (1)
Butter (2 Tbsp.)
Crumbled bacon (6 slices)

How's it done

1: Take out the Instant Pot and turn it on. Heat up the butter and once it is melted, add in the chopped onion, cooking to make tender.

2: At this time, add the parsley, pepper, salt, and half the chicken broth. Add the steamer basket inside and add the potatoes to the basket.

3: Place the lid on the Instant Pot and cook on a high pressure. After five minutes, release the pressure naturally and take the steamer basket out.

4: Add in the cornstarch and water mixture and stir around. Add the cheddar cheese, cream cheese, corn, bacon, cooked potatoes, half and half and the rest of the chicken broth.

4: Heat this all up so that it comes to a boil. Turn the Instant Pot off and transfer this over to serving bowls before enjoying.

Chicken Tacos

What's in it

Taco seasoning (1 Tbsp.)
Salsa (1 c.)
Water (.5 c.)
Chicken breasts (3)

How's it done

1: Place the chicken inside of your Instant Pot along with the taco seasoning, salsa, and water.

2: Place the lid on top of the Instant Pot and let it cook on a high pressure. After fifteen minutes and then use quick pressure release to let it all out.

3: Take the lid off the Instant Pot and then shred the chicken with two forks and stir it around. Add to your favorite shells or to some lettuce and serve.

General Tso's Chicken

What's in it

Sesame seeds (1 Tbsp.)
Cornstarch (2 Tbsp.)
Minced garlic cloves (2)
Grated ginger (.25 tsp.)
Red pepper flakes (.25 tsp.)
Hoisin sauce (3 Tbsp.)
Brown sugar (4 Tbsp.)
Soy sauce (4 Tbsp.)
Rice vinegar (6 Tbsp.)
Sesame oil (1 tsp.)
Cubed chicken (1.5 lbs.)
White rice, cooked (2 c.)
Chopped green onion (1)

How's it done

1: Turn on the Instant Pot and add in the sesame oil. Add in the chicken and let it cook for a few minutes.

2: While that is cooking, add together the garlic cloves, ginger, pepper flakes, hoisin sauce, brown sugar, soy sauce, and rice vinegar. Pour this over the chicken in the Instant Pot.

3: Add the lid to the pot and cook the chicken on a high pressure. After ten minutes, allow the pressure to quickly release from the pot.

4: Once you take the lid off, whisk the cornstarch inside and let it cook a bit longer.

5: Before serving, garnish with some green onions and sesame seeds and enjoy.

Spicy Moroccan Chicken

What's in it

Chicken stock (.5 c.)
Black pepper
Salt (1 tsp.)
Butter (1 Tbsp.)
Coriander (.25 tsp.)
Cinnamon (.5 tsp.)
Ginger (.5 tsp.)
Cumin (1 tsp.)
Garlic powder (1 tsp.)
Paprika (1 tsp.)
Chicken drumsticks (1 lb.)
Lemon zest (1 tsp.)
Lemon juice (1 Tbsp.)
Blackstrap molasses (2 tsp.)
Honey (4 Tbsp.)

How's it done

1: Take out a bowl and mix together the coriander, cinnamon, ginger, cumin, garlic powder, and paprika.

2: Using some towels, dry the chicken and then coat with the spices all over.

3: Turn on the Instant Pot and add in some butter. Place the chicken inside and brown it on all sides for about ten minutes.

4: Add in half a cup of the chicken stock. Secure the lid and then let this cook on a high pressure.

5: After ten minutes, you can turn the Instant Pot off and let the pressure out. move the chicken over to a bowl.

6: Mix together the lemon zest, lemon juice, molasses, and honey. Pour this into the Instant Pot and cook, without the lid on, for a bit longer to make it thick.

7: Use this sauce to coat your chicken. Serve with some green onions on top.

Beef Stroganoff

What's in it

Chopped white onion (1)
Sliced mushrooms (2 c.)
Olive oil (2 Tbsp.)
Cubed sirloin tip roast (2 lbs.)
Paprika (.25 tsp.)
Thyme (.5 tsp.)
Rosemary (.5 tsp.)
Garlic powder (.25 tsp.)
Onion powder (.25 tsp.)
Pepper (.5 tsp.)
Salt (.75 tsp.)
Flour (.75 c.)
Sour cream (.75 c.)
Beef broth (1.5 c.)
Minced garlic cloves (2)

How's it done

1: To get started, mix together the paprika, rosemary, thyme, garlic powder, onion powder, pepper, salt, and flour together. Add in the beef and toss it around to coat.

2: Turn on the Instant Pot and heat up some olive oil. Once this is hot, add in the prepared beef and brown it on all sides. You may need to do this in batches.

3: Add in the onions and mushrooms and cook before needing to add in the garlic.

4: Move the meet back to the Instant Pot along with the beef broth. Place the lid on the Instant Pot and cook at a high pressure.

5: After twenty minutes are up, turn off the Instant Pot and let the pressure naturally release.

6: Take the lid off and stir in the sour cream. Add some pepper and salt before serving over egg noodles.

Smoked Brisket

What's in it

Thyme (1 Tbsp.)
Liquid smoke (1 Tbsp.)
Chicken stock (2 c.)
Smoked paprika (.5 tsp.)
Onion powder (1 tsp.)
Mustard powder (1 tsp.)
Pepper (1 tsp.)
Salt (2 tsp.)
Maple sugar (2 Tbsp.)
Beef brisket (1.5 lbs.)

How's it done

1: Pat the brisket dry with a paper towel. Taking out a bowl mix the paprika, onion powder, mustard powder, pepper, salt, and maple sugar together. Use this to coat the meat all over.

2: Turn the Instant Pot on and grease it with some cooking oil. Add in the brisket and brown until it is golden and then flip it over.

3: Add the thyme, liquid smoke, and stock. Place the lid on top and cook at a high pressure.

4: After fifty minutes are done, take the pressure out and then take the lid off. Remove the brisket with some tongs and then cover with a bit of foil.

5: Let the sauces in the Instant Pot cook for a bit longer so that the sauce can thicken, keeping the lid off.

6: Slice up the brisket and then serve with the sauce and the veggies of your choices.

Instant Pot Hamburger Helper

What's in it

American cheese (4 oz.)
Cheddar cheese (16 oz.)
Heavy cream (8 o.)
Elbow macaroni (16 oz.)
Beef broth (2 c.)
Garlic powder (1 Tbsp.)
Onion powder (1 Tbsp.)

Ground beef (1 lb.)

How's it done

1: Turn on the Instant Pot to heat up a bit and add in the garlic powder, onion powder, and ground beef. Cook while crumbling up the meat and it is no longer pink.

2: Add in some heavy cream, the macaroni, and beef broth. Place the lid on the Instant Pot and cook on a high pressure.

3: After five minutes, turn the Instant Pot off and let the pressure slowly release.

4: Open up the lid and add in the American cheese and the cheddar cheese before serving.

Spiced Chicken Wrap

What's in it

Ground mustard (1 tsp.)
Ground cumin (1 tsp.)
Apple cider vinegar (3 Tbsp.)
Coconut oil (4 Tbsp.)
Chicken breast (1 lb.)
Romaine lettuce leaves (6)
Pepper (1 tsp.)
Paprika (1 tsp.)

How's it done

1: Take out a bowl and combine together the pepper, paprika, mustard, cumin, coconut oil, and apple cider vinegar.

2: Rub your chicken with some of the vinegar mixture, some oil, and the spice mixture and then let it marinate for half an hour or more.

3: When read, turn the Instant Pot on and add in the rest of the oil along with the chicken breasts. Cook long enough to brown.

4: Add in two cups of water to the pressure cooker and then turn to a high pressure. After twenty minutes, take the chicken out of the cooker and shred it up.

5: Take a piece of the lettuce and scoop some of the chicken on top. Sprinkle on the leftover vinegar and spices and then wrap it up.

6: Repeat the steps with the rest of the leaves and the chicken before serving.

Bacon and Chicken Meal

What's in it

Whipping cream (.5 c.)
Coconut oil (4 Tbsp.)
Bacon (.5 lb.)
Chicken breast fillet (1 lb.)
Prepared mustard (2 Tbsp.)
Butter (3 Tbsp.)

How's it done

1: To start, slice up the chicken breast into smaller pieces and then wrap each part with a slice of bacon.
2: Spray a baking pan with some cooking spray and then place the bacon wrapped chicken into the pan.
3: Take out the Instant Pot and turn it on. Add the oil and let it heat up before adding the bacon and chicken until they are browned.
4: While those are cooking, you can make the dipping sauce. To do this, melt the butter on the stove and whisk in the cream. Heat for a minute.
5: When this is warm, take it off the heat and add the mustard. Serve it with the bacon wrapped chicken and have a favorite side.

Cheesy Hotdog Huggers

What's in it

Cheddar cheese (2 o.)
Bacon (1 lb.)
Hot dogs (1 lb.)
Pepper
Salt
Onion powder (1 tsp.)
Garlic powder (1 tsp.)

How's it done

1: Turn on your pressure cooker to a high setting and add in two cups of water. Score the hotdogs with a slit going lengthwise.
2: Slice up your cheese into strips that are the length of your hotdogs and then insert them inside.
3: Wrap a slice of bacon around each hot dog and then seal with a wooden pick. Place these into the steamer basket inside the Instant Pot.

4: Place the lid onto the Instant Pot and seal it up. After about five minutes, quickly release the pressure and then enjoy.

3 SNACKS FOR THE MIDDLE OF THE DAY

BBQ Chicken Drumsticks

What's in it

Pepper
Salt
Minced garlic cloves (2)
BBQ sauce (2 c.)
Chili sauce (.25 c.)
Honey (3 Tbsp.)
Chicken drumsticks (1.5 lbs.)

How's it done

1: Take out the Instant Pot and turn it on. Add the pepper, salt, garlic cloves, BBQ sauce, chili sauce, honey, and chicken.
2: Close the lid and set to a low pressure. Cook this for about 2 hours.
3: Slowly release the pressure over a few minutes before taking the chicken out and serving.

Cocktail Meatballs

What's in it

Apple or grape jelly (1 c.)
Cocktail or chili sauce (.5 c.)
Meatballs (24 oz.)

How's it done

1: Turn on your Instant Pot to heat up. While this is heating up, mix together the chili sauce and the jelly.
2: Place your meatballs into the prepared Instant Pot and pour the jelly mixture on top.
3: Place the lid on top of the meatballs and cook at a high pressure.
4: After five minutes, turn the Instant Pot off and slowly release the pressure. Take the meatballs off and then let the sauce simmer a few more minutes.
5: Insert some toothpicks before serving.

Blue Cheese Beets

What's in it

Water (1 c.)
Crumbled blue cheese (.25 c.)
Pepper
Salt
Beets (6)

How's it done

1: Place the beets into the Instant Pot steamer basket. Add in a cup of water and cook on a high pressure.

2: After twenty minutes, let the pressure release naturally and remove the beets. When they have cooled down a bit before slicing into quarters.

3: Place the beets into a bowl with the pepper, salt, and blue cheese. Stir these together before serving.

Tomato Salad

What's in it

Pecans (2 oz.)
Cherry tomatoes (1 pint)
Sugar (2 Tbsp.)
Pepper
Salt
Pickling juice (2 tsp.)
Water (1 c.)
Apple cider vinegar (1 c.)
Goat cheese (4 oz.)
Sliced red onion (1)
Trimmed beets (8)
Water (1.5 c.)
Olive oil (2 Tbsp.)

How's it done

1: Put the beets into a steamer basket into the Instant Pot and add in the water. Place the water inside and then cook at a high pressure.

2: After twenty minutes, release the pressure and move the beets to a cutting board. Let these cool down a bit before peeling and chopping them out.

3: Clean out the Instant Pot and add in another cup of water along with the salt, pickling juice, sugar, and vinegar.

4: Cover the Instant Pot and let these ingredients on a high setting for another two minutes.

5: Release the pressure and strain out the liquid into a bowl. Add in the onions and lave alone for a few minutes.

6: Add the beets and the tomatoes and stir around. Add the pepper, salt, and olive oil and top with the pecans and goat cheese before serving.

Stuffed Bell Peppers

What's in it

Bell peppers, without tops or seeds (4)
Salt
Cumin (1 tsp.)
Garlic powder (1 tsp.)
Panko (1 c.)
Chili powder (2 tsp.)
Chopped jalapeno pepper (1)
Chopped green chilies (5 oz.)
Chopped green onions (2)
Water (1 c.)
Ground turkey (1 lb.)
Pico de gallo
Tortilla chips
Chopped avocado (1)
Pepper Jack cheese (4 slices)
Chipotle Sauce
Garlic powder (.25 tsp.)
Chipotle in adobo sauce (2 Tbsp.)
Sour cream (.5 c.)
Juice from a lime (1)

How's it done

1: Take out a bowl and mix together the garlic powder, lime juice, lime zest, chipotle in adobo sauce, and sour cream. Keep it in the fridge for a bit.

2: In another bowl, mix the garlic powder, chili powder, salt, cumin, jalapeno, bread crumbs, green chilies, green onions, and turkey.

3: When the second mixture is done, use it to stuff the prepared peppers.

4: Add some water to the heating up Instant Pot and then add the peppers to the steamer basket.

5: Cover the Instant Pot and cook on a high setting. After fifteen minutes, let the pressure release naturally for ten minutes and move the bell peppers to a pan.

6: Add the cheese on top and then place under the broiler until the cheese is browned.

7: Divide up the peppers and then top with the chipotle sauce and enjoy.

Tasty Sweet Carrots

What's in it

Water (.5 c.)
Butter (.5 Tbsp.)
Brown sugar (1 Tbsp.)
Salt
Baby carrots (2 c.)

How's it done

1: Take out the Instant Pot and mix together the sugar, salt, water, and butter inside. Turn the Instant Pot on and let these melt together.

2: Add in the carrots, stir things together and then cover the Instant Pot. Cook these ingredients on high.

3: After fifteen minutes have passed, release the pressure and take the list off. Let everything cook for a bit longer and then serve.

Cabbage and Sausage

What's in it

Chopped tomatoes, canned (15 oz.)
Sliced sausage links (1 lb.)
Pepper
Salt
Chopped cabbage head (1)
Butter (3)
Turmeric (2 tsp.)
Chopped yellow onion (.5 c.)

How's it done

1: Set the Instant Pot so that it starts to warm up and then add in the slices of sausage. Cook these until they become brown.

2: Drain out any grease that is leftover before adding in the turmeric, onion, pepper, tomatoes, salt, cabbage, and butter.

3: Place the lid on top of the Instant Pot and then cook on a high pressure.

4: After two minutes have passed, do a quick release of the pressure and then uncover the pot.

5: Divide up the sausage and cabbage before serving.

Eggplant Delight

What's in it

Pepper
Salt
Garlic powder (1 Tbsp.)
Minced garlic cloves (3)
Olive oil (1 Tbsp.)
Cubed eggplant (4 c.)
Water (.5 c.)
Marinara sauce (1 c.)

How's it done

1: To start this recipe, set the Instant Pot to heat up and add in the oil and the garlic. Cook for a few minutes.

2: Now add in the water, marinara sauce, garlic powder, pepper, salt, and eggplant. Place the lid on top and cook this at a high pressure.

3: After about 8 minutes, use the quick release method to let the pressure out and take the lid off.

4: Serve this eggplant mixture on its own or with some noodles for a great dinner.

4 DELICIOUS DESSERTS YOU ARE GOING TO LOVE

Banana Bread

What's in it

Baking powder (1 tsp.)
Mashed bananas (2)
Egg (1)
Vanilla (1 tsp.)
Soft ghee (.3 c.)
Coconut sugar (.75 c.)
Cooking spray
Water (2 c.)
Cream of tartar (1.5 tsp.)
Cashew milk (.3 c.)
Baking soda (.5 tsp.)
Salt
Flour (1.5 c.)

How's it done

1: Take out a bowl and mix together the cream of tartar and the milk. When those are combined, add in the bananas, vanilla, egg, ghee, and sugar.

2: In another bowl, mix the baking soda, baking powder, salt, and flour.

3: Now combine both of these mixtures and then pour it into the cake pan. Place the steamer basket into your instant pot and place the baking pan inside as well.

4: Add some water to your Instant Pot and then put the lid on top. Cook at a high pressure.

5: After thirty minutes, release the pressure and then take the lid off. Take the bread out of the Instant Pot and then let it cool down a bit before serving.

Apple Crisp

What's in it

Water (.5 c.)
Maple syrup (1 Tbsp.)
Nutmeg (.5 tsp.)
Chopped apples (5)
Cinnamon (2 tsp.)
Salt
Sugar (.25 c.)
Rolled oats (.75 c.)
Flour (.25 c.)
Butter (4 Tbsp.)

How's it done

1: Place your apples into the Instant Pot. Add in the water, maple syrup, nutmeg, and cinnamon.

2: In a separate bowl, mix the flour, salt, sugar, oats, and butter and stir well.

3: Drop some of this mixture on top of the apples and place the lid on top. Cook on a high pressure.

4: After eight minutes are up, let the pressure out and then serve this warm.

Chocolate and Pumpkin Cake

What's in it

Pumpkin pie spice (.75 tsp.)
Baking soda (1 tsp.)
Salt
Whole wheat flour (.75 c.)
White flour (.75 c.)
Chocolate chips (.6 c.)
Vanilla (.5 tsp.
Egg (1)
Water (1 quart)
Cooking spray
Pumpkin puree, canned (8 o.)
Greek yogurt (.5 c.)
Canola oil (2 Tbsp.)
Baking powder (.5 tsp.)
Mashed banana (1)
Sugar (.75 c.)

How's it done

1: Take out a bowl and mix together the pumpkin spice, baking powder, baking soda, salt, whole wheat flour, and white flour and stir it well.

2: Take out the second bowl and use a mixer to combine the banana, oil, sugar, egg, vanilla, pumpkin puree, and yogurt.

3: When these are both done, combine together your two mixtures, adding in the chocolate chips as you go.

4: Pour all of the ingredients into a Bundt pan and cover with some paper towels and foil. Place the steamer basket into the Instant Pot and add the Bundt pan.

5: Add some water to the pot and place the lid on top. Cook this at a high pressure.

6: After 35 minutes, start slow releasing the pressure and then take the lid off. Allow the cake some time to cool down before you slice it up and serve.

Holiday Pudding

What's in it

Chopped apricots, dried (4 oz.)
Water (2 c.)
Olive oil (1 Tbsp.)
Dried cranberries (4 oz.)
Grated carrot (1)
Eggs (4)
Maple syrup (3 Tbsp.)
Butter (15 Tbsp.)
Salt
Cinnamon powder
Ginger powder (1 tsp.)
Sugar (1 c.)
Baking powder (3 tsp.)
White flour (1 c.)

How's it done

1: Grease a pudding mold with some oil and then set to the side.

2: Take out your blender and pulse together the ginger, salt, cinnamon, sugar, baking powder, and flour.

3: Add the butter, eggs, and maple syrup and pulse in between each thing. Now add in the carrot and the dried fruits and let them fold into the batter.

4: Spread out this mix into a pudding mold and then add the steamer basket and two cups of water into your Instant Pot.

5: Place the pudding mold into the Instant Pot and then place the lid on top. Steam the pudding on a high pressure.

6: After 30 minutes, slowly release the pressure and then take it out to cool down a bit before serving.

Apple Cake

What's in it

Sugar (.25 c.)
Ricotta cheese (1 c.)
Water (2 c.)
Chopped apple (1)
Sliced apple (1)
Baking soda (1 tsp.)
Cinnamon powder (.25 tsp.)
Baking powder (2 tsp.)
White flour (1 c.)
Olive oil (3 Tbsp.)
Vanilla (1 tsp.)
Egg (1)
Lemon juice (1 Tbsp.)

How's it done

1: Bring out a bowl and add the sliced and chopped apples along with the lemon juice together before leaving to the side.

2: Take out a dish and line with some parchment paper. Add in some oil and dust with flour. Sprinkle the sugar on the bottom and arrange your sliced apples on top of it.

3: In another bowl, mix together the oil, vanilla, sugar, cheese, and egg and stir well. Add in the cinnamon, baking soda, baking powder, and flour as well.

4: Now add the chopped apple, toss around, and then pour it into the prepared pan.

5: Add a steamer basket to the Instant Pot and some water. Place the pan into the Instant Pot and cook at a high pressure.

6: After 20 minutes, let the pressure release, take the lid off the pot, and then serve the cake.

Pumpkin Pie

What's in it

Maple syrup (.75 c.)
Whole milk (1 c.)
Water (2 c.)
Eggs (2)
Chopped butternut squash (2 lbs.)
Chopped pecans
Whipped cream
Cornstarch (1 Tbsp.)
Salt
Powdered cloves (.25 tsp.)
Powdered ginger (.5 tsp.)
Cinnamon powder (1 tsp.)

How's it done

1: To start this recipe, place the cubes of squash into a steamer basket and then place into the Instant Pot. Add in some water and place the lid on top.

2: Cook these on a high pressure. After four minutes are up, turn the Instant Pot off and then release the pressure, moving the squash over to a strainer to cool down.

3: Mash up the squash a bit inside a bowl before adding the cloves, salt, ginger, cinnamon, eggs, milk, and maple syrup to it.

4: Pour this mixture into some ramekins and then into the steamer basket again. Add in some more water to the pot and cover it up, cooking at a high pressure.

5: After ten minutes, release the pressure and take the ramekins out. After they have some time to cool down, top with whipped cream and pecans before serving.

5 CONCLUSION

Thank for making it through to the end of this book, let's hope it was informative and able to provide you with all of the tools you need to achieve your goals whatever they may be.

The next step is to take out your Instant Pot and start using some of these great recipes in your own home. The Instant Pot is not just a great way to make meals quickly, it can be a great way to eat foods that are healthy and wholesome for you. This guidebook contained all of the great recipes that you need to eat healthily and get all the benefits that come from using the Instant Pot. So the next time you are looking for a tasty meal for your family, something good to fill you up in the morning, or even a good dessert everyone will love, make sure to pull out this guidebook and see just how great the Instant Pot can be, not only to save you time, but to help you eat healthy.

Finally, if you found this book useful in any way, a review on Amazon is always appreciated!

INDEX

Chapter 1: Wholesome Breakfast Recipes to Get the Day Started

Banana French Toast
Apple Oatmeal
Breakfast Cobbler
Egg Bake
Egg Muffins
Sausage Frittata
Tomato and Spinach Quiche

Chapter 2: Lunch Recipes to Help Keep You Full

Vegetable and Beef Soup
Chicken Noodle
Cheesy Potato Soup
Chicken Tacos
General Tso's Chicken
Spicy Moroccan Chicken
Beef Stroganoff
Smoked Brisket
Instant Pot Hamburger Helper
Spiced Chicken Wrap
Bacon and Chicken Meal
Cheesy Hotdog Huggers

Chapter 3: Snacks for the Middle of the Day

BBQ Chicken Drumsticks
Cocktail Meatballs
Blue Cheese Beets
Tomato Salad
Stuffed Bell Peppers
Tasty Sweet Carrots
Cabbage and Sausage
Eggplant Delight

Chapter 4: Delicious Desserts You are Going to Love

Banana Bread
Apple Crisp
Chocolate and Pumpkin Cake

Holiday Pudding
Apple Cake
Pumpkin Pie

Printed in Great Britain
by Amazon